# Creating An Ebook

## How To Create an Ebook For Beginners

By
Jasmine Baker

# Table of Contents

Introduction ........................................................... 1

Chapter One - Why Should You Write an Ebook? .............. 3

    Resources ...................................................11

Chapter Two - How to Choose a Fantastic Topic .............12

    Resources ...................................................30

Chapter Three - How To Write and Publish Your First
eBook ..................................................................31

    Deciding on the Ebook Format ...........................33

    How to Hire an Ebook Writer for Ebook Creation..........35

    Resources ...................................................36

Chapter Four - How to Write Your Ebook in 24 Hours or
Less! ................................................................. 37

    Resources ...................................................45

Chapter Five - The Most Effective Ways to Make Your
Ebook More Valuable ............................................. 46

    Resources ...................................................51

Chapter Six - Beginner's Guide to Creating an Ebook in
Simple Steps ....................................................... 54

    Resources ...................................................59

Chapter Seven - How to Get Rid of Writer's Block in Easy
Steps ................................................................ 60

    What is the definition of writer's block?..................60

    How to Get Rid of Writer's Block in Easy Steps..............61

    Resources ...................................................68

**Chapter Eight - Writing an Ebook - Mistakes Made by Ebook Writers That Keep Their Ebook From Selling ....... 69**

Resources ...................................................................................77

**Conclusion............................................................................ 79**

# Introduction

Congratulation! If I hadn't done it for myself, I wouldn't have believed it. It is possible to write an ebook without really writing it. You can hire a writer and then hold the whole copyright to the work after the writer is completed, according to a unique legal twist. It's almost too wonderful to be true if it sounds too good to be true!

But there's another benefit that's almost too good to be true: writing an ebook is a fraction of the expense of writing a hardcover book. It's actually rather reasonable for someone who intends to return their investment through ebook sales.

Another almost-too-good-to-be-true fact: ebooks frequently sell for the same price as physical books!

**It's not a problem if you don't know how to write.**

Allow me to tell you a little about my story. Dollar signs flashed almost constantly in the back of my head as the Internet began to take over the world. I performed some investigation to find out who was profiting from the evolution. I discovered importers, search engines, online development/hosting companies, and auction websites. It had been a year since then. The Internet is beginning to define business more than ever before. For their listening pleasure, people are really paying for and downloading tunes. People are using the internet to plan, research, and book entire holidays. The Internet is inhaled by those who adore information. There is information all over the place.

That, of course, creates a dilemma. Excessive amounts of information. Part of the problem with Internet research is that the information you gather while surfing is disorganized, if not completely disorganized. You go to Google and look for something. You observe that thousands of pages are relevant to your search terms. As a result, you refine your search by adding a few words. You're down to a few hundred pages now. And then you start clicking on them one by one.

Then there's the issue of up-popping popups. Those pesky creatures. By the time you close all the windows, you may have forgotten why you sat down at the computer in the first place.

Even on sites without pop-ups, you have no idea what you're going to get or whether the source is trustworthy. As a result, the Internet is a feast, with some of the possibilities spoilt. Yuck! However, because the buffet is so appealing, most of us return to try our luck again and again.

Anyway, all of this made me wonder about ebooks. Sure, you can read Charles Dickens on a computer, but what I'm talking about is nonfiction ebooks that teach. If I could put a few decent ebooks online, individuals who wanted to learn more about a subject could read a full book from a reliable source online.

So I gave it a shot. What's more, guess what? I didn't have much luck at first. But I got back up, studied, and tried again, and again, and again. I eventually found a formula that worked, primarily through trial and error.

Although this book was written after all of that, I believe it is past time for me to share my experience. On the Internet, there is enough room for everyone. Take a seat!

# Chapter One - Why Should You Write an Ebook?

E-book marketing has exploded in popularity over the previous decade. Consumers now have access to e-books everywhere because of the tremendous sales of tablets, smart phones, and e-readers.

Experts expect that digital reading will supplant traditional print in the not-too-distant future. This projection is like money in the bank for entrepreneurs who are already promoting online.

An e-book is the most effective technique to promote your business if you have a website with a high-quality product for sale. It's an opportunity to share your unique message with the world and establish yourself as an authority on your subject.

An e-book, whether utilized as a promotional freebie or as the main event in content marketing, can help your website's SEO and brand recognition. Additionally, an e-book might help you engage with current consumers or attract new ones. Your readers are more inclined to buy from you if they believe the information you're passing along is reliable and will assist them in solving an issue.

**The following are the top reasons to write an e-book for your business:**

## 1. Generate Targeted Leads

Ebooks can assist you in attracting qualified leads. The explanation is simple: when you give something worthwhile in return, people will happily give you their contact information. These are the people who are interested in your services or products. You can educate them and convert them into paying clients if you write it well.

## 2. Establish yourself as an Expert

You'll have a plethora of knowledge, experience, and skills to contribute no matter what sector or industry you're in. You can establish yourself as an authority in that sector by publishing it as an ebook.

A best-selling author with a series of novels, for example, will undoubtedly establish himself as an expert.

Furthermore, ebooks might help you establish credibility and trust. People will always look to you as the leader or someone to whom they will resort when they have a question about the issue.

## 3. Outperform the competition

The corporate world is becoming increasingly competitive. So, what makes your target audience pick you over one of your competitors?

If you're a tiny business, creating ebooks is a smart decision because your competitors are (probably) not doing so. You will have the first-mover advantage and will be able to reach out to a specific audience.

It provides a new way to promote your business in addition to regular social media posting, email marketing, and blog posting. Don't let this opportunity pass you by.

## 4. Increase the number of visitors to your website

You may start promoting your ebooks on social media to drive traffic to your website, blog, or product page once you've finished creating them. Remember to add a call-to-action in your books, directing readers to your website, a sale page, or mobile apps, for example.

## 5. Create a bond with your audience by interacting with them.

The value of having an email list for long-term business success cannot be overstated. As a result, providing your audience with an eBook is the most effective strategy to expand your email list. Before mailing them the ebook, get their email address.

It's a fantastic time to start creating a relationship with them and collect some feedback now that you have their emails. You can do a lot more with your audience if you're innovative.

## 6. Easy to create

Ebooks are really simple to create, and they cost nothing but your time.

Creating eBooks does not necessitate any specific abilities. You may make your own ebooks with a variety of free resources available online. Simply compose your material in a Word or PowerPoint document and save it as a PDF.

## 7. Establish a Passive Income Stream

Though making money from eBooks may not be your primary motivation for writing them, selling them can provide a steady stream of cash.

If you want to start a publishing company like me, you'll need to write a lot of eBooks. You can't just rely on a book.

## 8. Being an eBook Creator is simple.

All you really need to get started is a word processor and an idea. Most computers currently come with software that includes a good word processor, a spell checker, and the capacity to count words. Many of them will also run a grammatical check on you.

## 9. You can become an eBook creator in a short period of time.

You'll need a concept and the desire to write about it. You may create an eBook in as little as a couple of days with a little effort. Within a week, for sure. It will take more time to research if it is a subject you enjoy or have always wanted to learn more about. Alternatively, you can hire ghost writers or purchase a PLR product to compensate for your lack of writing prowess.

## 10. Any eBook that has been created can be delivered instantaneously.

Your eBook is capable of being sent at the speed of light. It might be anywhere in the world where there is access to the Internet or a cell phone connection. That leaves around 1.5 billion Internet users and 5.0 billion phone users as potential clients.

## 11. As an eBook creator, your return on investment (ROI) might be extremely high.

You've probably heard that doing something once and getting paid again is one of the finest ways to make a lot of money. That is what your eBook creation entails. With the correct topic matter and well-written material, it can last for years.

## 12. Selling your eBook creation might be a pretty straightforward process.

You'll have several alternatives for selling your eBook creation. If you have or plan to create a website, you may make it simple for people to download the eBook from there. If you wish to charge for it, you can utilize PayPal and charge a little fee for customers to pay with credit cards. Then there are the big players like ClickBank and Commission Junction, where you may sell your eBook not only alone, but also through a network of affiliates that can help you grow your business tenfold.

### 13. When you publish an eBook, you establish credibility for yourself.

Who would you go to first for advice? Someone who is currently conversing with you? Or perhaps someone you've seen on the front cover of a book? I think you'll agree that you'd like to hear from the person represented on the cover of that book.

### 14. It's a fantastic approach to grow a marketing mailing list.

If you've ever considered doing business on the Internet, you've probably heard the phrase "The Money is in the List!"

And this is the list they're referring to. You'll be able to make a wonderful payday by pressing a button and sending an email to a list of people who are interested in those types of things as you grow a list, or two, or three.

### 15. Creating a foundation for back-end sales

You can transfer customers who like your items up the market scale as you progress from an article to an eBook to a series of videos, MP3s, CDs, and maybe DVDs. This is where the "gurus" get their six- and seven-figure earnings. You can also utilize your eBook as a reason for people to join your mailing list at no cost to you.

### 16. The initial investment necessary to start a productive firm is really minimal.

Starting an online eBook creation business might be quite inexpensive. Depending on what you want to achieve, you can start with as little as $50.00 To $200.00. You can start your business even if you don't have access to a computer. Most public libraries now have free computers that you can use. And as your business grows and your success grows, you'll be able to afford those really wonderful things you'll need to run your business more comfortably (not to mention those types of expenses could be tax deductible to reduce your costs further.)

## 17. Can build an army of affiliates to boost revenue with minimal additional cost.

Wouldn't it be great if you could get 10, 20, 100, or 500 people to help you sell your eBook for FREE? It's simple to do this with ClickBank or Commission Junction. (There are others, but these are the two most important.) More information can be found at http://www.cj.com/ and http://www.clickbank.com/.

## 18.You can create an eBook on nearly any topic.

You can write on whatever subject you desire, but you should consider what will give you the most chance of being profitable. How do you know if a subject will be profitable? Do a Google search for it to check if anyone else is selling something related to it. If there are ads on the side and top of the first page, someone is making money there since people do not pay for advertising unless they are selling something to pay for it.

## 19. eBooks created can be used to build your own viral marketing system.

Writing a valuable eBook with active links to your site or affiliate site can be given up for free and encouraged to be shared with others. As the book is distributed and spread among friends and acquaintances, you will be able to develop a viral marketing campaign that will cost you very little money, if anything at all, other than your time.

## 19. Created eBooks, like articles, can live on the Internet for a long time.

(Let's call it a baker's dozen.)

When you search for certain terms, you will come across articles from the last 4-5 years. The third piece, which I was looking for research material for, was in its fourth year of being on the first page of Google.

# Resources

Copyblogger: A blog with great tools for creating ebooks, articles about content marketing, and podcasts about writing.

Copyscape: A website to check writing for any signs of plagiarism.

CoSchedule Headline Analyzer: A tool to write SEO-friendly headlines with emotional impact.

Headline Analyzer: Analyzes headlines for SEO and compelling words.

Hemingway Editor: Points out long, overly complex sentences.

Grammarly: A tool to correct grammar and spelling mistakes.

Readable: A tool to determine how readable your writing is.

RefDesk: Helps you make sure your facts are straight.

Title Cap: Tells you if a word should be capitalized.

Title Generator: Helps you generate solid titles for SEO.

# Chapter Two - How to Choose a Fantastic Topic

Choosing an ebook topic has never been easier. People are hungry for information, and the Internet serves as a source of such information. After reading this chapter, you'll be confident enough to choose your own topic, or you may simply copy and paste your ebook topic from this ebook! So, how's that for a bargain?

**Keep an eye on what's going on around you.**

If you're intelligent enough to read this book, you're also intelligent enough to examine your surroundings and identify what interests you and people around you. Consider the difficulties you've recently solved, as well as the problems others have encountered and solved. Any difficulty you've overcome in your life might easily become the focus of your future book. People enjoy reading about how others have addressed problems similar to their own.

So, make a list of issues that you and those around you are dealing with. Bob, a buddy of yours, has lost his job? Is it true that your sister's child had chicken pox? What strategies did they use to cope or find solutions? While you're at it, make a new list of unsolved problems that you've noticed in your area. Make a list of problems you wish you could have fixed. Ahha! These are themes that will pique people's curiosity! How to get rid of those final ten pounds? The real story regarding UFOs. The most direct route to millionairedom. From your own vantage point, your step-granddaughter is 14 years old and pregnant? Is your grocery bill more than double what it was before? Do you have a leaking roof? These are issues that need to be solved with an ebook!

These unsolved issues might make excellent ebook subjects. Remember, you only need to know the issue, not the solution. You're going to hire someone else to conduct your research and write your book. You will not be writing a single word.

## Goggling for a few minutes

The Internet is an excellent resource for learning what people are seeking at any given time. Almost anything may be searched for. **You can use GoogleTM or any other popular search engine, such as Yahoo!® or Mamma.com.** Enter terms like "top American concerns," "best-selling nonfiction topics," or "popular how-to books" into the search box. 2005's most common concerns

## Also, while you're on the web...

Use the New York Times bestseller list, Amazon, and a Google search for ebooks to find the most popular nonfiction books. Your data will reveal exactly what book topics individuals are currently purchasing.

Give it a shot. Go to www.amazon.com for more information. Click "Top Sellers" from the tabbed menu at the top of the Amazon home page.

In September 2008, I performed this and came across a Harry Potter book, numerous other fiction books, and titles like Natural treatments "they" won't tell you about, How what you wear may transform your life, How to benefit from the dollar's destruction, and The official SAT study guide. To some extent, I've paraphrased, but you get the point.

Here's what I discovered after just a few minutes on Amazon that day. People are reading good fiction by authors who are already best-selling (Da Vinci Code, the Harry Potter series, and others). Second, Amazon consumers are interested in nonfiction themes such as improving their lives and generating more money when they shop on the internet. Any author will do for these works, even complete unknowns or people who have served time in prison for lying to the American public.

And that little visit just proved that the nonfiction ebook industry is the most direct path to ebook income. This is due to a variety of factors. The majority of fiction readers prefer to snuggle up in a chair with a real book. Some of them go to book clubs, when tangible volumes are brought to a person's kitchen table along with wine and cheese. Readers of fiction prefer to buy from authors they are already familiar with. Writing and delivering well-written fiction can be more difficult. Many of the great works of literature are also available as free ebooks. Those could easily be downloaded by a fiction reader. So, unless you're feeling exceptionally daring and experimental, stick to nonfiction.

Here's some more wonderful news for you, and if you didn't already know, you're going to be overjoyed. Please hold your breath... ideas are not trademarked. Therefore, you can use any idea you see, hear, or read anywhere, at any time, for an ebook! You can write books based on the same concepts as those found on Amazon's best seller list, then turn around and publish an ebook on the same topic!

Now, because copyright law protects how ideas are conveyed, you'll want to make sure your hired author doesn't plagiarize or replicate the book text verbatim. You can't even use the title word for word. However, nothing prevents you from writing a second book or ebook about the same subject in a different voice. It's all as legal and guilt-free as nonfat cheese. Haagen Dazs is a popular ice cream brand. Looking at bestseller lists is a wonderful technique to gain topic ideas in this case.

## Taking it a step farther

Hobbyists are one type of people who are eager to buy nonfiction ebooks. These people are always looking for new ways to spend their money on their hobbies. Their motivation is to help you make money.

Search the web for "popular hobbies," "enthusiasts," or "what America is buying" to find hobbyists and niche organizations. You can also look for hobbyist-specific forums and discussion groups. In the forums, people converse with one another in order to share ideas. They frequently trade endorsements for equipment, future events, and books.

Yahoo! is a popular platform for enthusiasts to communicate with one another online. Take a look at it. Go to www.yahoo.com for more information. Go to "groups" and select it. You'll find a range of categories on the groups page, such as Business & Finance and Religion. Click on "Games" for demonstration purposes.

The game subcategories are listed on the game screen, followed by numbers. The numbers represent the number of discussion forums available in that subcategory. These figures reveal a great deal. Take note of how "role playing games" and "video & computer games" have ten or even 100 times the number of forums as other categories. "Wargaming" and "paintball" aren't even close, despite the fact that those topics generate far more debate than "horseshoe pitching."

One day, just for fun, I kept selecting subcategories until I had a list of over a thousand (yes, a thousand) Yahoo discussion groups devoted to vampire role playing. This is how I arrived: World of Darkness>>Vampire: The Masquerade>>Games>>Role Playing Games>>Live Action>> World of Darkness>>The Vampire: The Masquerade

New members are welcome to join some of the forums, and you can read what everyone is talking about. You can review conversation topics from today, yesterday, or a year ago after you've entered the forum. If you want to learn about the trendiest conceivable ebook subjects, don't go too far back. If you want to, you can participate in discussions. If you join a discussion group just to promote an ebook, hobbyists will consider you spam and will remove you from the group.

You'll find out what this group is buying if you read and/or participate. You only have to browse over the pages to see what questions they're asking each other about items, vacations, and information. Because enthusiastic buyers prefer to research before they buy, knowing what they're interested in buying is crucial knowledge. This is a hot ebook market right now. Create a book about how to choose the greatest of this or that on the market, based on current enthusiast desires.

Enthusiasts come in a variety of sizes and shapes. Brides-to-be, golfers, whitewater rafters, vintage baseball card collectors, wine enthusiasts, gardeners, frequent vacationers, video gamers, and parents who enroll their children in private tutoring, ballet, and violin classes before the age of three are just a few examples.

Playing golf, watching football, renovating vintage automobiles, and listening to music are just a few of the hobbies that seem to keep attracting newcomers. These are timeless classics. Some hobbies, such as Red Hat Society membership, snowboarding, and line dancing, appear to come and go in waves. For the best odds, choose a traditional interest or a fluctuating hobby during its peak season.

The Internet has a large market for people in their 20s and 30s. According to one survey, this is what they are doing right now. Snowboarding, wakeboarding, traveling, camping, listening to music, and taking photographs are among their favorite pastimes. They enjoy rock climbing, playing guitar, camping, dancing, online dating, purchasing computers and other electronic devices, attending sporting events, studying the Bible, exercising, looking for work, and watching movies. Any of these topics would make a fantastic ebook, and there is a ready market for it.

## How-tos and hot topics

How-to books have essentially no limitations in terms of marketability. Everyone wants a how-to handbook, **advice**, and confidence that they can accomplish anything they read in a how-to book. Any skill you have, any skill you've always wanted to learn, or any skill that can be taught can be turned into a how-to ebook.

How-to books for hobbyists are a good place to start, and this tie up with the previous discussion. A hobby how-to guide could cover everything from constructing a hay bale home to learning how to play Texas Hold 'Em poker to comprehending Shakespeare.

Knowing how hungry we are for how-to information, one book publisher has designed an entire series of "Dummies" books for the market. There are other **other** book series that are comparable to this one, and they are all doing well! The "Everything" and "Idiot's Guide" series, among others, are cashing in on the how-to craze.

You might make money by writing ebooks on any or all of the topics covered in those series. Check out their catalog of titles at www.dummies.com. Choose one that appeals to you and go for it!

Remember that, despite the title, the novels are so successful because the readers are not treated like dummies at all. The authors are writing for someone who wants to know the simplest method to do something without getting bogged down in irrelevant details. When you're writing your ebook and choosing a title, make sure you're appealing to a reader's intellect! If you use adjectives like foolish, dumb, or hopeless in the title, make it clear that the meaning does not include insulting the reader personally.

Because of their brevity and the fact that they are sold exclusively through the Internet, ebooks can reach a smaller audience. It is not necessary to write a general book such as

How to Use a Computer (which may not be interesting enough to sell anyway in this decade). Ebooks can cover a broader range of topics. **Knowing this, you may 1) tailor your ebook to a certain niche audience, and 2) build more ebooks covering different aspects of the same subject and sell them independently!**

Assume you've decided to publish a fishing ebook. (It's worth noting that this is one of those hobbies where devotees are willing to spend money!). "How to Catch Freshwater Trout," "How to Tie Your Own Flies," or "How to Plan a Successful Deep Sea Fishing Trip" are all possibilities. Depending on how much information you offer, almost each aspect of the hobby can be turned into a distinct booklet. Clearly, "How to Put on Waders" would be a poor pick (though some would argue that underestimating today's **consumer** is impossible), because you'd have to work hard to fill 60 to 100 pages on such a simple topic. You get my drift. In most circumstances, the topic would have to be worthy of a book. Use your best judgment.

Then, as we know from "Life's Little Instruction Book," life itself necessitates instructions. As a result, life is a good theme for a how-to book. There are so many subtopics to choose from that you'll never run out of ideas. Listed below are a few examples:

- "How to ensure your child gets an A+ in math"
- "How to have a successful garage sale"
- "How to organize your home office"

While we're on the issue of how-to books, I'd like to bring up one thing. These ebooks' titles don't have to be very smart. Make sure the words "How to" appear first in the title, and the rest of the title should clearly state what the ebook is about.

**Which of these three titles, for example, would be the best?**

- "How to have a successful garage sale."
- "One weekend away from a cleaner house"
- "How to sell your old shoes for a profit"

Despite the fact that numbers 2 and 3 are intelligent, a touch punchy, and correspond to the ebook content, I still recommend title number 1. "How to have a successful garage sale" puts it up nicely and will capture the eye of an Internet surfer looking for a how-to manual on how to organize a garage sale.

Anyway, let's get back to the topic at hand. A how-to book can be about any stage of life, technique of coping with life, or huge or minor aspect of life.

## Looking young

Although sixteen-year-old girls may not wish to seem younger, looking younger is a frequent desire for the majority of the population in Western society after that. Everyone is looking for the fountain of youth, whether it's in the form of a medication, a particular diet, surgery, or an ebook.

An ebook about how to stay or look young as you become older will have a bright future. Here are a few title suggestions; I'm sure you can think of a lot more.

- "Drop ten years and ten pounds in ten days"
- "How to look 28 forever"
- "100 ways to look younger"
- "Grocery store products that will help you look younger"
- "Look 30 again without surgery"
- "How to live to be 100"

This is a really heated topic. Baby boomers, the elderly, and even ladies as young as 20 are purchasing Botox, surgery, chemical peels, lasers, diets, acupuncture, electronic pulses, mega vitamins, prescription teas, thigh cream, and teeth whiteners! Nobody wants to appear to be a day older than they are.

## Health

Everyone is concerned about their health, whether they are growing old or unwell, have experienced illness with a loved one, or simply desire more energy. You should make a solid investment in health ebooks. Doctors aren't required to be the authors. Anyone with any credentials or none at all, can write a health book. Just make sure you're not claiming to be a doctor unless you are.

Here are several health-related topics that will almost certainly generate quick attention, reading, and sales!

**Preventing and curing diseases.** Most of our baby boomer generation will develop heart disease, cancer, diabetes, dementia, or some other ailment as they age. Give these people some reason to believe. Create an ebook about how to deal with stress, how to identify the best practitioners, how to prevent disease causes, or remedies that American doctors aren't aware of.

**Natural remedies.** People are interested in herbal, natural, and holistic treatments as alternatives to conventional medicine. Make a book about any disease that includes alternative treatments. "How to Treat Lymphoma Naturally," for example. You might also simply talk about natural supplements in general, such as "The greatest natural cures for common disorders" or "Holistic health."

**Diet.** What we consume is usually a topic of discussion. There are dozens, if not hundreds, of diet fads out there right now. You can make an ebook out of any of them. Obesity, overall health, and diet supplements such as vitamins are important factors to consider. Consider the question, "How to set up your kitchen for a macrobiotic diet." "Eat to cure cancer," as the saying goes.


## Travel

Never before has there been so much travel available to so many people. People nowadays desire to communicate with the people they care about. They wish to go to other parts of the globe. See unusual sights. Allow yourself to be entertained. Also, because adults, particularly in the United States, frequently work more than 40 hours each week, individuals require excellent vacations. They're doing their homework to ensure that they get the most out of their limited vacation time each year.

Here are some ideas for you: how to swap frequent flyer miles, how to avoid airport security, how to travel on a penny and earn change, and how to keep your kids entertained on long vehicle rides.

There's plenty of room for publications like the finest amusement parks for your money, top 100 campgrounds, things to see and do in Utah before you die, and free things to do in Washington, D.C., in addition to how-tos.

Have you gotten the picture? The benefit of writing travel ebooks is that you may already know a lot about a location that other people might want to visit. It's a breeze!

## Money

Money (along with the earth's axis and planetary forces) keeps the world spinning, so it's no surprise that ebooks on the subject are plentiful. They do, but the market isn't even close to being fully saturated. More can always be added. People are constantly interested in how-to books about money, from becoming wealthy to simply saving money on a daily basis. Below are some suggestions:

- "How to feed your family on less than $40 a week"
- "How to get free stuff"
- **"How to pay almost no taxes"**
- **"How to buy a retirement home for no money down"**
- "How to be richer than your parents"
- **"How to buy cars at auction"**
- "How to start a financial management business"

## Enrichment of life

Despite the fact that fewer and fewer people are attending churches these days, an increasing number of people are rushing to bookstores to buy self-help books. Self-help books are flying off the racks at traditional bookshops. People want to believe that by reading a self-help book, they can alter their lives completely. Whether or if this is correct is irrelevant. Changing your life, investigating your spirit, and assisting yourself are all excellent ebook subjects.

People want to know how to make peace with their pasts, how to be creative or spiritual in a consumer world, and how to discover true love now more than ever. You might write an endless number of how-to books on the subject of self-help or life enrichment. Here are a couple more ideas:

- How to marry for life
- How to unbreak your heart
- How to stay sane in a crazy world
- How to meditate

## A few more topics bound to explode

These are smoldering hot topics that are only going to get hotter. You can choose any of these to use as the basis for your first ebook. Then return and select a new topic for your next ebook.

**Using the latest electronics.** We live in a society that is preoccupied with having the most up-to-date technology. Make an ebook about iPods, email/camera phones, wireless Internet, digital television, or any combination of these.

**Home improvement.** This is such a rage that do-it-yourself (DIY) stores may be found on every corner in large cities. You are one of the rare people who hasn't visited a Home Depot or Lowe's recently. Apartment dwellers and young students aren't in this market, but people who own homes and have the financial means to do so are. In fact, several cable TV providers have specific channels for home improvement.

In-home automation systems are a hot topic right now. DIY home improvement enthusiasts are ready to learn about and purchase items that will make their lives at home more relaxing, high-tech, or enjoyable. Make a book to educate them how to turn on their lights before they arrive home from work, or how to alter their window blinds, music, or temperature with the touch of a button. Or, to put it another way, how Bill Gates' residence operates. Or how to retrofit an old home with automation, or how to incorporate automation into the design of a new home.

**Identity theft prevention.** This is an excellent topic, especially since ebooks are sold through the Internet. This is due to people's concerns that their credit card data will not be seen by others or misused in any way when they shop online. Consumers are concerned about identity theft even when they are not using a computer. People nowadays shred their receipts, remove their personal information off the face of their checks, and conceal their faces with their hands when typing passwords at public terminals or ATMs. ID cards are being implanted with microchips. The public is concerned. Use an ebook to tap into this!

Safety. People are concerned about their safety from crime, chemical warfare attacks, and natural disasters, in the same way that they are concerned about identity theft. If you watch the evening news tonight, you'll be able to come up with at least twenty things that people are scared about. When you discuss safety, you are conversing in their language. Titles like "Be Prepared for Any Natural Disaster," "Never Be a Crime Victim Again," "How to Defend Yourself in a Parking Lot," and "Prevent Sudden Infant Death Syndrome" would be popular (SIDS).

How-to guides for every new product that has recently been released. This is similar to the Dummies series, except it goes a step beyond. People who want to buy the most recent commercially available item should read your ebook. How to operate the latest John Deere tractor type. You'll know that no one else has a book like yours, and you'll be able to boast about it in your sales presentation.

How to get through any stage of life. As people go about their daily lives, they are confronted with a variety of demons and struggles. When many people are in need, they will turn to others for assistance. Support groups, private counseling, spending time with friends, and starting afresh are all good ideas for an ebook. You could also reach out to specific people who require emotional support. How to get through the dreaded adolescent years. What to do if you've been told you've been diagnosed with cancer. Having to deal with my own flaws. What is the best way to live with someone who is dying? Getting through high school. Any of these options will suffice.

Anything that has to do with pets. People are lavishing more attention on their pets than ever before. Some pets are given preferential treatment over humans. People who spend little fortunes on their dogs will be willing to pay a high price for an ebook that gives them advice on how to treat their pets even better than they already do.

Write books about how to care for your parakeet, how to prepare homemade meals for picky dogs, where to find pet spas, how to raise your children to be cat-friendly, million-dollar mutt homes, which animals make the best pets, or pet psychology.

Traveling was intertwined with the previous topics. People not only want to travel like crazy, but they also want to tailor their itineraries and travel methods to their passions and lives. Try a few of these out for size: places to eat throughout the world while sticking to a low-carb diet. Hotels with the best fitness centers. How to travel with giant dogs with style. Make your campsite crime-free. Be inventive. Here's where you'll find a market.

Meeting individuals via the internet. As I have stated, the mania has arrived. Everyone is online these days, and some people spend more time communicating with their online pals than they do with their real-life friends. I'm sure I've been guilty of it myself. Anyway, the World Wide Web brought with it folks who needed a little help figuring out how to get where they wanted to go. They're looking for like-minded folks, a date, love, and support.

There is a sizable ebook market dedicated to connecting people online. Speed dating online, virtual music jams, online classes, hooking up with individuals who share your hobby, and discovering online support groups are just a few examples of topics that could be covered. Any of these, as well as others, are of interest to those who want to make the most out of their ability to network with people in the farthest regions of the globe, owing to the Internet. Indeed, one of the benefits of online communication is that distance is irrelevant. With an ebook, you can assist these people in faraway nations in finding each other.

Topics that are particularly interesting to women. The facts are unmistakable. Women are the most active users of the Internet, spending or influencing 80 cents out of every $1 exchanged. For business owners and authors, what women want has never been more crucial.

Certain themes are particularly appealing to women. Beauty, health, decoration, emotional support, and life enrichment are among them. In general, women do a few things that men do not. They play bunko, put on make-up, and talk on the phone for hours with their girlfriends. They send more cards, make more casseroles, and vacuum more frequently than men. They eat more salads and shop for clothes more frequently. They enjoy getting pedicures and dancing more than ordinary men.

When it comes to women and ebooks, there are two things to bear in mind. If you want to appeal to a female audience, you should write about a topic that women enjoy reading about, and the title should be female-friendly.

Where to discover amazing shopping discounts in Taos is a female-oriented theme and title. And here's one for the guys: Where in Taos can you catch the most fish?

Where to locate amazing shopping discounts in Taos is a female-friendly title (same as above). And here's a title on the same subject that's more suited to men: Keep your money in your pocket in Taos. Do you see the distinction? Know your market, and if you have to choose between the two, the women's title is the safer bet.

Sex. People are well aware that they no longer need to smuggle sexual publications out of bookstores. They're looking for sex materials, toys, and novels on the internet. Individuals can take their sweet time on the Internet, and they can even surf with or without a partner sharing their chair. Orgasms for Two is a new ebook that has been a big hit. More comparable ebooks are required. On the theme of sex, a fiction novel may also be effective. You may write sensual short stories or an ebook on how to have excellent sex. Adults who are interested in this genre would enjoy either of these ebooks (and incidentally, most adults are indeed interested in this category).

## Resources

Creatavist. Lets you integrate text, audio, video, and interactive elements into ebooks, and then publish for iPad, iPhone app, Kindle, Nook readers, and Web.

Dribbble: Portfolio site/place to find freelance designers.

FlipHTML5: Tool to make interactive ebooks, including images, links, buttons, videos, slideshows, and more.

Kotobee: Ebook creator to design and publish interactive ebooks in minutes.

KitPDF: Converts ebooks into a readable file across different devices.

My eCover Maker: Tool to make 3D ebook covers.

Pexels: Site for free high-quality stock photos.

PressBooks: Easy service to create and format an ebook, including ebook design templates and customizable themes.

Sigil: A free, open-source WYSIWYG ebook editor.

Unsplash: Site for free high-quality stock photos (10 new photos every 10 days).

# Chapter Three - How To Write and Publish Your First eBook

It can be intimidating to write your first eBook. It undoubtedly appears to be near-impossible. However, the truth is that you do have a book inside of you. You have an eBook that can be utilized not simply to promote your business, but also as an additional source of revenue that, with some thought and planning, can grow into many more.

## Come Up with an Idea

The first business eBook you publish might serve as a vehicle for expressing your basic principles as a business owner or for imparting knowledge to others. If you have a thriving business, for example, you may relate the tale of how you built it and provide suggestions **with** others on how to achieve the same.

## Creating an Outline

An outline should be the first step in writing any eBook (as well as any article or blog). For this outline, you don't need to care about your form. You're merely utilizing it to organize and collect your thoughts. Write a working title, then topics you want to discuss that become chapters, then a synopsis of what you want to say in each chapter, and finally an outline for each chapter.

## Don't Be Concerned About Errors

When you initially sit down to write your first lines (and, in fact, the entire first rough copy of your novel), the smartest thing you can do is focus on the task at hand rather than on whether or not you're making mistakes. Write in the same tone as you speak. Don't try to pass yourself off as someone else. Any problems will be resolved during the editing process.

**Begin with a blog.**

Blogging the book first is one technique for writing an eBook. Then, with the help of an editor, you may put it together, adding transitions and other information as needed to finish the project.

**Make Small Goals**

One page every day may be excessive. Instead, you might wish to set a time restriction for each writing session you schedule. You want to set tiny goals that are achievable but not so small that you don't make progress toward your dream of finishing a book.

**Get a Professionally Designed Cover**

Don't cut corners on the cover. Hire someone with a strong portfolio of covers you like. Make sure the cover you've created is suitable for both print and digital media.

**Amazon's Kindle Publishing**

You don't need a traditional publisher these days to make it a reality. Today, many people begin by self-publishing, and if you have an audience, a publisher will not be turned off if you have a large audience. They'll find their way to you. Today, Kindle makes it simple to publish, and it also allows you to offer print-on-demand copies, which you should take advantage of.

## Deciding on the Ebook Format

Your ebook can be downloaded in a variety of formats. So, once you've finished it, consider how you might make it available to people in the manner that most suits them.

**The following are the most frequent ebook formats:**

**PDF** – The most well-known and accessible format for readers is PDF, which stands for 'Portable Document Format.' It allows you to insert hyperlinks, interactive text, and graphic information into practically any desktop or mobile device or software.

**EPUB** (Electronic Publication Format) - EPUB (Electronic Publication Format) is a collection of HTML files that provide many different degrees of formatting control and require specific expertise (or apps) to generate. They can only be accessed using specialized software like Apple iBooks or a web browser that supports this format. Fixed layout and reflowable EPUBs are the two types of EPUBs.

The fixed layout is similar to PDF, which allows for hyperlinking and rich visual formatting based on a text layout that remains constant as the screen changes. Reflowable EPUBs, on the other hand, work like web pages that adapt to different mobile devices and tablets. However, for more advanced visual styling, they demand additional XML/HTML knowledge.

**MOBI -** Amazon bought the Mobipocket Reader program that created the MOBI format in 2005, but it was shut down in 2016. Despite this, it is still a popular ebook format that works with most ereaders (excluding the Nook). Audio and video are not supported by MOBI.

**AZW -** AZW is an ebook format created by Amazon for the Kindle, although it is also supported by a wide range of smartphones, tablets, and PCs.

**ODF –** OpenDocument format) is a file type used by OpenOffice, which is an open-source content creation tool similar to Microsoft Office.

**IBA -** The IBA format is an ebook format that is only compatible with Apple's iBooks author software and not with any other ereader. Video, sound, pictures, and interactive media are all supported.

Among these, the MOBI format, as well as PDF and EPUB, are the most commonly used file formats.

However, which one (s) you choose is determined by the ebook authoring program you use and the distribution channel you prefer. Canva and Visme, for example, let you download your ebook as a PDF file, but InDesign lets you export your manuscript as an ePub file.

So, before you choose which one to utilize, make sure you consider all of your options.

# How to Hire an Ebook Writer for Ebook Creation

There are a variety of reasons why you might require an eBook yet not desire to write one yourself. In general, hiring an eBook writer is a good idea if you want a free offering that is better written than what you can offer but still relevant to your niche.

There are various options for hiring an eBook writer, but the most straightforward is to use work-for-hire websites. Start by going to a website like Get A Freelancer, Elance, or Guru. You can post your eBook project on these websites, and freelance writers can bid on it, and you can choose a writer for your e-book.

To get started, you'll need to pick a site and establish an account. After you've completed this, you'll be able to publish your eBook project. Include the type of e-book you want, the title, table of contents, or niche market, as well as any other details you've previously figured out. The more specific you are, the lower your bids will be, and your writer will have less work to accomplish.

You will be able to post a budget for the project, with a range of how much you are willing to spend. If your budget is tighter than the budget ranges allow, you should be more explicit in your project description. Include the time frame or turnaround time you anticipate for the book's completion.

Freelancers will be able to bid on your job after it has been uploaded. It is ideal to find an e-book author who has already received feedback or reviews and can provide some form of sample writing. Choose the writer with the lowest bid, the fastest turnaround time, and the best writing skills.

## Resources

ClicktoTweet: Lets readers tweet snippets of your ebook.

Hootsuite: Manage up to 35 different social networks. Customize your feed, schedule posts, and track analytics.

MailChimp: Create multiple lists and segments for targeted email marketing.

SlideShare: Upload and share your PowerPoint presentations, ebooks, Word docs, or Adobe PDF portfolios.

Tweetdeck: A customizable dashboard that displays timelines, trends, hashtags, and more.

Alltop: An aggregator of the Internet's most popular stories.

Answer the Public: Visualizations of the questions people ask Google.

Brainpickings: An inventory of cross-disciplinary interestingness, spanning art, science, design, history, philosophy, and more.

BuzzSumo: Insights on the most-shared content on any topic.

Brandwatch: Find out what web users are reading and writing related to specific keywords.

# Chapter Four - How to Write Your Ebook in 24 Hours or Less!

Is it possible to write an eBook in less than 24 hours? It isn't possible. After reading the title of this post, you're probably thinking something similar. The truth is that many writers have created ebooks and special reports in less than 24 hours.

The qualifier comes first. I mean 24 hours of writing and editing when I say 24 hours. Not for 24 hours straight...unless you're a glutton for torture or have already written a large first draft, writing a draft in 24 hours will be difficult, very difficult.

The purpose of this part is to demonstrate that if you figure out how to write faster, the sky is the limit in terms of what you can accomplish in terms of growing your publishing empire. The second goal is to provide a few methods for getting your writing done quickly.

To be successful, you should utilize the checklist below to generate a first draft in a short amount of time.

## 1) Keep it short, sweet, and to the point.

Keep your ebooks short and to the point if you want to write quickly, especially if you're just starting out. You want to be able to answer your reader's questions as quickly as possible.

Keeping your ebooks short is the best approach to coming up with a rapid solution. In my special reports or short ebooks, I try to aim for 25 to 40 pages.

What is the distinction between a special report and a brief ebook?

There isn't much difference between them; in fact, they are one and the same. What you call it depends on your niche and marketing strategy.

If you want to create some excitement around something, calling it a special report might attract you a little more attention than calling it an ordinary ebook.

## 2) Stay Focused

When writing a brief report, it's critical to keep on track and avoid getting off track. Make sure you go over your study and eliminate anything that isn't focused on one subject and one subject only.

If you try to answer a lot of questions or address a lot of problems, the pages will start to add up, and your first draft will quickly go from focused to bloated.

You'll complete faster if you stay focused on a narrow issue. Allow your topic to grow and you may never be able to finish it.

## 3) Simple Steps and Secrets

A well-written outline or table of contents will aid you in staying on track and completing your first draft in a timely manner.

My go-to method for coming up with interesting chapters and themes is to make a list of the actions required to solve the problem or attain the outcomes I'm writing about.

Take, for example, an e-book plan on how to write an ebook. I know it's ironic, but here's how the 7 Steps Outline works:

- About the Author
- Introduction
- Overcoming Your Excuses
- Step #1 - Niche It
- Step #2 - Research It
- Step #3 - Table It
- Step #4 - Write It
- Step #5 - Edit It
- Step #6 - Polish It
- Step #6a - Re-Edit and Re-Polish
- Step #7 - Publish It
- The Next Steps in Your Journey
- Exclusive Interviews with 8 Successful eBook Authors
- Conclusion

I can just construct multiple sub-topics under each stage now that I have my blueprint. I'll think about what has to be done throughout each step and write a few paragraphs under each sub-topic before moving on to the next sub-topic.

## 3) Sizzling Sexy Chapters

Make sure your chapter names are attractive and attention-getting, which is another must-follow suggestion. People will be more engaged and more likely to read your ebook, which is one of the key reasons you're writing it in the first place.

Another advantage of incorporating several chapters is that each stage or secret can begin with a new chapter on a new page. Even if you don't write any more, this increases the length of your first draft automatically. This leads us to the mystery of...

## 4) White Space

You'll notice that there aren't many lengthy paragraphs in some of your favorite ebooks if you flip through them. This is due to the difficulty of reading large amounts of text on a computer or portable electronic reading device.

Adding some white space, such as a space between paragraphs, big pronouncements, or quotes, will not only make your ebook easier to read, but will also boost its size. The larger product will be interpreted by your readers as a value for the amount you will be charging.

## 5) A Captivating Title

It's no surprise that titles like The Automatic Millionaire, The One Minute Millionaire, The One Minute Manager, Eight Minutes in the Morning, and Eight Minute Abs are used in books and goods.

Think Eight Minute Abs, not How to Work Out Endlessly and Get Nice Abs! Create an eye-catching title that immediately emphasizes the advantage the reader will receive.

## 6) Getting Unblocked from Writer's Block

You may not have taught your thoughts and fingers to start writing as soon as you sit down at the computer when you initially started writing on a regular basis. Here are a few techniques to jumpstart your writing if you're having trouble finishing your first draft.

## 7) Review Industry Headlines and Reports or Articles

Simply go to your niche-specific news resource or forum online if you're stuck on what to write next about a topic or sub-topic. Many websites offer a search function that you may use.

Turn off your computer. Reading on a computer all day and then trying to write on a computer might be challenging at times. Unplug and go offline is my recommendation. Look for books or articles regarding your eBook topic in your local library or at a nearby bookstore. Look over the table of contents or read a chapter or two to get ideas for your eBook.

You now have some new thoughts and approaches to your issue. You might even have a book or two that you can use to quote or reference in your own work. Another quick technique to obtain content is to utilize a quote and then remark on it.

I only have one word of caution for you: do not plagiarize. Read through the information, think about it, and then write about it in your own words.

## 8) Seek Assistance

Another excellent method for completing your writing is to hire someone to do it for you. Yes, I realize that this defeats the purpose of learning how to write your own first draft, but if you're having trouble writing an ebook, you can always hire someone to do it for you.

Getting a ghostwriter to create your eBook for you is what outsourcing your project entails. A ghostwriter is a person who works behind the scenes and will write your manuscript for you for a fee. The cost is determined by the scope of work, which includes the number of pages, the topic, and other factors.

Using a ghostwriter has the advantage of allowing you to concentrate on the creation of your website and sales copy while your ghostwriter works on your product. This is one of the ways you can become an author right now.

Another alternative is to produce your own ebooks by repurposing other people's words. Taking use of other people's knowledge. Allow me to explain...

## 9) Interviews

This method is still effective, although it has become a touch overused in the internet marketing sector in recent years. You approach specialists in your field and conduct interviews with them. You record the interview and then transcribe it yourself or hire someone else to do it for you.

You can even have the person you're interviewing respond to questions by email, leaving you with nothing to record.

This method has the advantage of allowing you to tap into the expertise of recognized specialists. When you publish your product, they may be prepared to market it to their list of subscribers as an added benefit.

Imagine publishing an eBook and having thousands of people visit your website the day it is released, thanks to a recommendation from a niche expert.

Of course, the entire procedure can be done in less than 24 hours, which means you'll be able to complete your first draft in under 24 hours. That's not awful at all.

## 10) Ebooks in the Public Domain

You can also use public domain material as a final resort. A literary work in the public domain is copyright-free, which means you can use it in any way you wish.

**There are three types of public domain works:**

Because the author gave the information, it is now publicly available.

Governments and their agencies provide information.

Works that became public domain after the author's copyright was lost

When you're looking for public domain literature to publish, the final scenario is arguably the most common. In general, any work created prior to 1923 is considered part of the public domain.

So, how do you go about turning public domain texts into ebooks? You simply locate the work and transcribe it, or you locate the raw file and convert it into a first draft. How can you locate a work in the public domain?

I did it one of two ways: using Google and entering in "public domain" and the topic I'm interested in, or going to Gutenberg.org and visiting Project Gutenberg. Gutenberg is a fantastic resource for locating hundreds of public domain books that you can use to create your own ebooks.

So there you have it: just a few techniques to write your first draft in under 24 hours.

# Resources

Discover: Tool to help discover inspiration, research opportunities, and collaborate with your team.

Feedly: Aggregates content from your favorite publications, blogs, and keywords.

FiveThirtyEight Newsletter: News, statistics, and trending topics.

Forekast: A real-time record of upcoming events and holidays.

Google Trends: Tracks trending subjects.

Oz Content: Software to help you generate data-informed content ideas by consolidating research and ideas.

Portent's Content Idea Generator: Generates ideas based off of keywords.

Scoop.It!: A site to help you find great content that you can put a spin on to publish at a later date.

Trendspottr: Shows emerging trends and pre-viral content.

Ann Handley's Blog: Great tips from a great writer.

# Chapter Five - The Most Effective Ways to Make Your Ebook More Valuable

So, you've just finished your eBook's basic outline. You've come up with a unique and valuable product to offer people in your niche. However, you are attempting to answer the following question in the back of your mind:

How can I increase the value of my eBook to the customer?

What can I do to differentiate myself from how everyone else is promoting their eBooks on the internet?

The following are the first measures to consider while adding value to your eBook:

## The Topic

Make sure you know anything about the subject of your eBook or have an interest in it. This is an important aspect of making your product relevant and instructive to the customer. While creating your topic, you should also consider what your target market wants and needs to know. You can be sure that you're identifying the needs of your target niche if you do it this way.

## The Length

When it comes to deciding the length of your eBook, there are no hard and fast rules. With less than 20 pages, some eBooks can be informative and useful. Don't obsess over any kind of word limit that has been set. On the other side, make sure you're continually presenting your customers with helpful and important information. Use no fluff or filler to stretch your text to a given length. Present your data in a clear, well-organized, and succinct manner.

Many people mistakenly believe that an eBook's value is determined by the number of pages it contains. This is untrue; an eBook's success and profitability are determined by the quality of content offered to the customer.

## The Title

The eBook industry is extremely competitive, so you'll need to stand out from the crowd. While a headline like "5 strategies to acquire a free cell phone from the government" can make for an excellent 500-word article, it lacks the "rock and roll" essential to pique readers' interest and produce a "wow" effect.

## The Content

If you've been writing for a while, you're probably aware that you need to have unique and fascinating material if you want people to read what you have to say. This is when your knowledge and enthusiasm for your niche come into play. You must present your readers with information that is not available in other eBooks.

This means that if you're producing an instructional or a "how to," you should do some research on the competition and avoid regurgitating the same content over and over again. You might discover that your content is obsolete, useless, or simply incorrect. Write in simple terms for the average person (or woman) and include examples. Being distinctive and original is a big part of increasing the value of your eBook.

## The Editing

If your eBook offers ground-breaking, useful, and important material that has never been published before, but it has apparent grammatical faults, it will fail. To ensure that your eBook is up to standard, either proofread it thoroughly or employ a professional editor. Otherwise, the reader would assume that the author was simply unprofessional or clumsy, and that the content is flawed.

## The Cover Design

Developing an appealing cover design after you've finished writing your content is a way to add value to your eBook. When it comes to developing your eBook, the old adage about judging a book by its cover is regrettably extremely true. You may miss out on a huge portion of the market if your cover isn't eye-catching and unique.

Unless you are a professional designer, you should hire someone who has previously created vibrant, fascinating eBook covers. On the internet, there are a plethora of low-cost cover designers to choose from. Custom eBook covers are available from Elance and Killercovers, both of which provide a no-questions-asked money-back guarantee.

## The Target Market

Finding and identifying a core market and focusing your eBook on meeting their needs is far more useful. It all boils down to getting your eBook in front of the correct audience. For example, if you're writing about "the finest balance transfer credit card deals for 2012," you probably don't want to target a market that is concerned about the environment;

while you might get a few purchases, your long-term worth will suffer.

## The Selling Price

If this is your first foray into the world of eBook sales, you'll want to make sure your product is priced fairly. You can raise your pricing if you've had some success and built a following. People are constantly on the lookout for bargains, and eBooks are no exception.

Some folks are willing to offer a 100-page eBook for under a dollar. This method will dramatically improve your eBook sales and reviews on sites like Amazon, allowing you to climb the bestselling book ladder while also raising the value of your product through word of mouth marketing.

On this point, I need to provide further information. While there are several schools of thought on charging less to get your e-book out there and charging more to make people believe they are getting high-powered information that costs more, there are several schools of thought on charging less to get your e-book out there and charging more to make people believe they are getting high-powered information that costs more. Every method isn't appropriate for every product. You should conduct niche research to determine where the gaps in your intended e-book audience are and charge appropriately.

Now that you've covered the fundamentals of adding value to your eBook, I'd want to go over some more advanced ideas for ensuring that you've developed a professional and saleable eBook, as well as how you may monetize that content.

It makes no difference whether you're creating an eBook for profit or to provide a bigger service or product to your audience. For you, the ultimate product must be appealing, valuable, and profitable.

So you've completed a 100-page eBook with original, high-quality content. You can put what you've written into a series of high-quality videos using what you've written.

You now have not only an amazing 100-page eBook, but also a video series to go along with it. You can keep going by converting the e-book to an audio book. And now you've got:

- A 100-page eBook, 20 videos, and 15 audios are included.

Because you're offering more, you may now raise your selling price. You might also write "cliff notes" with a one- or two-page summary of each e-book chapter, then post this information on a members-only blog for your members to ask questions about. After that, you can interview some people in your niche who you respect and appreciate for more content. And once you've completed that, you'll have plenty of leftover knowledge to create another series about what you've learned along the road. You now have:

- Includes a 100-page eBook and 20 videos 15 audio files There are 13 cliff notes. There are ten master class interviews and 30 pages of tips and tactics gained along the road.

Your original eBook's worth has significantly increased. You may now develop an upsell by offering email coaching for $$$ per month, weekly coaching calls for $$$ per month, and so on.

After that, you may figure out what the most prevalent issues are among your audience and construct a teleseminar to address them. You may host a live event for your clients and hire someone to film it so that you can sell DVDs or stream the footage afterwards.

## Resources

### PublishXpress

PublishXpress is an online conversion tool that takes DJVU, DOCX, TXT HTML, RTF and PDF files and converts them into MOBI and EPUB. This is perfect if you already have your e-book ready and just want to turn it into both MOBI and EPUB so it can be available to other e-book readers. The service is free, but watch out for any imperfections in your converted text.

### Zinepal

Similar to Papyrus but with a dated interface, Zinepal also allows you to turn blog posts into content for your e-book. You can also start from scratch. Just note that the free account will put a Zinepal link on the bottom of each page of your book.

### Google Docs

A simple way of writing and converting content into PDF online for free is by using Google Docs. Type in your content and have all the Google Fonts available for you to choose from all inside the Google Docs window.

It syncs with your Google Drive account, so you can work on it from any device as long as you're online.

# Desktop tools to write/create an eBook

## Scrivener

Scrivener is an advanced writing software for authors who write novels and screenplays. To create an e-book, you need to enter your content just like you would a regular book. When you're done, use the Compile feature to export it to e-book formats like MOBI, EPUB and Kindle. It's not a very simple process, but there are great tutorials online on how it's done.

## Calibre

Calibre is primarily a free e-book management software and e-book viewer, so you can store e-books and organize them into a library, but it also converts between PDF, EPUB, MOBI and other e-book formats. Converting e-books within its user-friendly dialog is great for beginners, and there's a lot of changes you can make to your converted piece.

## iBooks Author

iBooks Author is an e-book editing software for making books to sell exclusively on Apple iBooks. The format will only work for Mac and the iPad. While this might seem restrictive, keep in mind that some readers prefer to read on their iPads because of the clear retina display, so making your ebook with iBooks Author is going the extra mile for your future readers..

## Microsoft Word

Anyone with a PC will be familiar with MS Word, so creating an e-book using this software is great for those who don't want to learn another software.

If you have the Microsoft Word 2016, you can convert your DOC file to PDF within MS Word without having to purchase an add-on. However, there are dozens of DOC to PDF converters online which you can use for free.

## Kindle Gen

Kindle Gen is a command line app for converting HTML or any other e-book source into the Kindle e-book format (for selling on Amazon). If you're familiar with using the command window, then this tool is not that difficult.

## Adobe InDesign

If you're familiar with the Adobe Creative Suite, using InDesign should be easier for you. Otherwise, you may need to go through some tutorials before using this tool. InDesign is a more advanced method of creating an e-book and it's mostly if you want the graphics and all style elements in your e-book look polished and professional.

## Open Office

While Microsoft Word is commonly used, Open Office is completely free to use and it converts .doc to .pdf without having to pay a single cent. Since it's very similar to Word, you'll be typing your content and be done in no time. When you're done writing and proofing your content, simply click on *File>Export to PDF* and you're done.

# Chapter Six - Beginner's Guide to Creating an Ebook in Simple Steps

## Step #1: Write Your Ebook Content

Without content, an ebook would not exist.

The content for your ebook can be created in two ways. You have the option of repurposing previously published content or creating something entirely fresh.

Make sure that anything you choose resonates with your current and potential customers. The fundamental goal of offering an ebook is to provide value while also solving a problem. Of course, the subscribers you earn are fantastic.

Knowing who you're writing for will make the process of creating content a lot easier. Send the text to your target customer. Use the same language that your clients do to ensure that they get the material fast.

Keep it short, avoid fluff, and avoid using too much technical language. You're on the right track if you can imagine people nodding their heads while they read.

Make the appropriate quantity of research to provide the best information to your audience. Check everything for accuracy and cite any sources you have.

The title should be attention-getting, informative, and completely cover the subject. Avoid using esoteric metaphors or clumsy language. Before they download your ebook, readers need to know what they're getting.

## Step #2: Organize Your Content

Before you start developing your ebook, it's a good idea to divide your content into sections. Each section of a good ebook will contain a table of contents with descriptive titles. These should only contain a few words, just enough to make each point obvious.

## Step #3: Use Your Style Guide

If you're making an ebook for your company, you probably already have a style guide. Request a style guide from a client if you're developing an ebook for them.

These will save you time and allow you to focus on creating amazing content. You can quickly customize your Visme Brand Kit with your own fonts, colors, layouts, and logos, and then use it to build your ebook.

Choose sections of the text that can be converted into bullet points or graphs. Look for interesting paragraphs that can be made into infographics.

Make a note of any passages that could be used as subtitles or quotes. These can visually break up big blocks of text, allowing the reader to skim the content before reading it.

All of your text should be edited and proofread. Even if the information is carefully written, grammatical errors and typos will make it appear unprofessional. For assistance, use online editors like Grammarly, Hemingway, or Prowritingaid.

Before you go into a designer, make sure you've thought through your page layout, especially when it comes to the mobile devices your ebook will be read on, whether they're Android or Apple smartphones, ereaders, an iPad, or anything else.

## Step #4: Choose Images and Create Visuals

It's time to develop the visuals now that you have the text, a rough notion of how the parts will be organized, and a style guide. When choosing imagery for an ebook, the most important thing to keep in mind is balance.

To add visual value to your information, use the Visme editor to create charts, maps, graphs, and diagrams. But don't go overboard — just enough visual interest to pique the reader's curiosity.

There should be a nice mix of content and graphics on each page of the book. To utilize in your ebook, you may quickly add your own photos to the Visme library. There are also a lot of free photos inside the editor that you may utilize.

## Step #5: Design Your Ebook

It's now time to put everything together and create your ebook.

Start by looking through our list of ebook templates below to see what might work for you.

## Step #6: Publish and Share

It's time to make your ebook available to your audience after it's finished. Will you give it away for free in exchange for email subscriptions or sell it on your website?

Visme allows you to download your ebook as a PDF file, which can then be shared easily online. You may also make interactive ebooks and embed them on a website or share a Visme-hosted online link.

## Step #7: Promote Your Ebook

What good is it to spend all that time and work creating and designing an ebook if you don't promote it? Aside from the registration or buy now buttons on your site, don't forget to use social media to promote your business.

Create some social media visuals using the same style guide as the books. Create an ebook cover design and utilize an online mockup generator to create a professional-looking image.

Distribute them in places where your readers congregate. Draw their attention to your e-book by demonstrating how it will address their problem. Send an email to your list of subscribers with a link to the e-book download. Request that they forward it to any friends who might be interested.

Create Facebook Live videos and Instagram Stories to promote your new ebook. Show your followers the table of contents and tell them a little about what's within. Make an animated video to attract more attention.

Create an article about your ebook on your blog. On your homepage, promote your ebook. Request testimonials from some of your readers and put them in the post.

You might also make a landing page with the ebook cover, a brief description, and a sign-up form. A website exit pop-up could be a good idea as well. Read this article to learn how to create effective exit pop-ups.

When optimizing your landing page, keep SEO in mind to ensure that Google properly indexes and ranks your ebook.

**Step #8: Select the Appropriate Ebook Software**

This is by far the most important of all the steps in this quickstart tutorial. You won't be able to publish and promote your ebook unless both the content and the design are of high quality.

This is why it's critical to use the correct ebook software so you can quickly create a visually appealing ebook that your readers can't wait to get their hands on.

Visme is an excellent ebook software program for writing material, putting it into a professionally designed template, dragging and dropping your own visuals and data visualizations into it, and then downloading and sharing it with your audience.

# Resources

Smashwords Style Guide – Complete formatting instructions

Creating ePub files with Apple Pages for iBookstore – from Apple

Kobo for Authors and Publishers – the Guide to publishing on Kobo

Barnes & Noble Pubit! ePub Formatting Guide – Downloads the PDF

Calibre Manual – Contents for this popular e-book management software

Amazon Kindle Publishing Guidelines – How to use the Kindle Platform

Bookbaby.com guidelines for e-book conversion – a new service with a unique approach.

Amalthia's e-Book formatting tutorial – pages of instruction

The ABCs of e-book format conversion: Easy Calibre tips for the Kindle, Sony and Nook – tons of helpful tips

Getting Started With Google eBooks – The lowdown on publishing to Google's eBookstore

# Chapter Seven - How to Get Rid of Writer's Block in Easy Steps

If you've ever experienced writer's block, you know how frustrating it can be – it can prevent you from writing for days, weeks, or even months. While it may be tempting to ignore the problem in the hope that it will go away on its own, writer's block is one of those bugs that requires active management.

## What is the definition of writer's block?

Writer's block is a condition in which you are unable to continue writing and/or begin writing something new. Some people feel it's a real illness, while others say it's all in their heads. Regardless, we can all agree that writer's block is a terrible and tough condition to conquer.

You might wonder what causes writer's block. Clinical psychologists Jerome Singer and Michael Barrios decided to find out in the 1970s. They discovered four broad causes of writer's block after tracking a group of "blocked authors" for several months:

- Self-criticism that is excessively harsh
- Fear of being compared to other authors
- Lack of external motivation, such as praise and attention
- Internal motivation, such as the desire to convey one's tale, is lacking.

To put it another way, writer's block is caused by a variety of feelings of dissatisfaction with the creative act of writing. But don't worry, these sentiments aren't permanent! After all, every writer starts with a sense of purpose and anticipation; overcoming writer's block is all about regaining those sentiments. Let's have a look at some of our suggestions to see how you can do that.

## How to Get Rid of Writer's Block in Easy Steps

### Establish a writing schedule.

"Creativity is a habit, and the best creativity is a product of strong work habits," author and artist Twyla Tharp famously said. To others, this may appear counterintuitive. Isn't creativity something that ebbs and flows organically, not something that you can plan for?

But the truth is that if you just write when you're "in the mood," you'll end up in a quagmire of writer's block. The only way to get over it is to discipline yourself to start writing creatively on a regular basis. It may be every day, every other day, or only on weekends - whatever it is, make it a habit!

### Use words that are "imperfect."

A writer can spend hours searching for the right word or phrase to convey a message. Put "In other words..." and just write what you're thinking, whether it's eloquent or not, to avoid this useless (and block-inducing) exercise. You may then narrow it later by searching for "in other words" with CTRL+F.

## Participate in non-writing activities

One of the easiest methods to get out of a writing rut, according to children's book editor Maria Tunney, is to step away from your own work and into someone else's:

"Go to an exhibition, the movies, a play, a concert, a nice dinner... immerse yourself in amazing STUFF and your synapses will crackle in a new way." Snippets of speech, noises, colors, and sensations will infiltrate the once-empty space. Perhaps you'll be able to return to your work with a fresh sense of purpose."

## Freewrite through it

Freewriting entails writing without stopping for a predetermined amount of time — with no care for grammar, spelling, or topic. You simply write.

Of course, what you scribble down may or may not be related to your present endeavor, but that's okay! Freewriting's purpose is to write without second-guessing yourself – to write without uncertainty, indifference, or self-consciousness, all of which contribute to writer's block. To get started, follow these steps:

Look for the right environment. You should go somewhere where you won't be disturbed.

Choose your writing implements. Will you write with a pen and paper or type on your computer? (Tip: if you're prone to using the backspace key, freewrite the old-fashioned way!)

Set a time restriction for yourself. Set your timer for 10 minutes the first go around to get a feel for it. As you become more comfortable with freewriting, you can progressively extend this interval.

**Take it easy on your first draft.**

Perfectionism is a common problem among authors, and it may be especially crippling during the first draft. Lauren Hughes, the editor, says:

"Writers frequently have blocks because they place a lot of pressure on themselves to sound 'perfect' the first time. Allowing oneself to write imperfectly is a terrific approach to loosen up and have fun again in a draft."

Remember that "perfection is the enemy of good," so don't sweat the small stuff! You can always go back and make changes, or have a second set of eyes look over the manuscript. However, for the time being, simply putting the text on the page will enough.

**Do not begin from the beginning.**

The beginning is by far the most scary portion of writing, when you have an entire book to fill with coherent words. (It makes us break out in a cold sweat just thinking about it.)

So, rather than starting at the beginning of whatever it is you're trying to write, start in the middle or wherever you feel comfortable. Because you're "already at the halfway point," you'll feel less pressure to get everything "perfect" right away — and you'll be all warmed up by the time you return to the beginning!

## Take a shower

This isn't a recommendation for personal hygiene. Have you ever observed that your best ideas come to you while you're showering or performing other "mindless" activities?

There's a logical reason for this: studies demonstrate that while you're doing anything repetitive (like washing, walking, or cleaning), your brain goes into autopilot mode, allowing your unconscious mind to wander freely without being constrained by logic. To put it another way, you're more able to fantasize and create creative connections that you might have missed otherwise. Simply lather, rinse, and repeat until the block has been kicked to the curb!

## Keep your inner critic in check.

The inner critic, oh, the inner critic! With a heavy dose of self-doubt, you can always bring your work to a halt. You'd be hard-pressed to find a writer who hasn't been stymied by their inner critic, as Stephen King, Margaret Atwood, and Charles Bukowski all experienced it.

Successful authors have the capacity to listen to their inner critic, acknowledge its criticisms gently, and go forward. You don't have to dismiss that critical voice entirely, nor should you be afraid of it. Rather, you must build a polite, balanced connection so that you may focus on the important issues while ignoring the insecure and unnecessary ones.

## Change up your tool.

A change of location can help with writer's block, as you may already know. That landscape doesn't have to be your physical location, though; switching out your writing tool might be just as beneficial!

Try moving to pen and paper if you've been typing on your word processor of choice. Consider adopting specialized book writing software if you're tired of Google Docs. (We recommend the Reedsy Book Editor, which has a built-in goal reminder system that you can turn on if you find yourself slipping behind on your writing schedule!) Even the tiniest change can have a significant impact on your productivity.

## Alter your point of view

"When you're stuck, attempt to imagine your tale from another perspective 'in the room' to assist yourself go through the block," says editor Lauren Hughes. What would a minor character say if they were watching the scene? Is that a 'fly on the wall' or something else inanimate?

"Changing your perspective for a short time can offer you 'fresh eyes,' allowing you to identify the parts in the picture where you can improve and how to move from there."

## Exercise your creative muscles

If you want to get better at something, you have to practice it, and writing is no exception! So, if you're feeling stuck, it could be time for a strengthening scribble session to help you out. To get started and inspired, look through these lists of creative writing prompts, writing exercises, creative writing examples, and writing tactics.

**Create a story map.**

If your story has stalled, take a more structured approach — particularly, write an outline — to help it pick up momentum. Not only can figuring out your story's trajectory address your current problem, but it will also prevent future problems!

**Experiment with a more visible method.**

When words fail you, forget about them and focus on your vision. Make mind maps, drawings, or Lego buildings - whatever that helps you clear your head, as long as it's linked to your tale.

You may also try the Inkflow software, which functions like a visual word processor and allows you to effortlessly move and doodle on your ideas. This software might become your new best buddy if you're the type that likes to outline by sticking sticky notes on the wall.

**Create a story map.**

If your story has stalled, take a more structured approach — particularly, write an outline — to help it pick up momentum. Not only can figuring out your story's trajectory address your current problem, but it will also prevent future problems!

**Compose something new.**

Though it's crucial to try to get through writer's block with the project you're currently working on, it's not always possible. If you've been beating your head against your story for a long time, put it aside for the time being and start writing something fresh.

**Turn off the computer.**

It's a little miracle that authors can get ANYTHING done on machines that are meant to connect to a world of distraction. Try a site blocker like Freedom or an app like Cold Turkey if willpower isn't your strong suit and staying focused is your biggest difficulty. The latter is a particularly cool remedy to writer's block in that it converts your computer into a typewriter until you meet your writing objective, leaving you with no choice but to write.

**Allow the words to discover you.**

Allow the words to find you when you can't find them! To start the words flowing, meditate, go for a stroll, take the shower we mentioned, or (the constant refrain) use an app.

## Resources

**Best Places to Hire Ebook Ghostwriters**

Upwork

Freelancer

Fiverr

Textbroker

Constant Content

PeoplePerHour

Toptal

HireWriters

Guru

# Chapter Eight - Writing an Ebook - Mistakes Made by Ebook Writers That Keep Their Ebook From Selling

The ability to write and sell an eBook on the internet has transformed the publishing industry. Rather than waiting one to two years to compose and publish your work, you may now have an eBook produced and ready to sell on the internet in a matter of weeks, if not days. However, many authors make the same mistakes time and time again, resulting in their eBooks not selling as well as they had intended. When writing an eBook or other information product, people commit the following mistakes.

Not conducting preliminary research to determine how many individuals are searching for information on your particular issue. It makes no difference whether you believe your idea would make a good eBook or not. What counts is that thousands of other people are looking for information on your subject on a regular basis. To check how many people are searching for the words that describe what you've written about, use Wordtracker or one of the other free keyword search engines.

Trying to market an eBook that focuses on what people need rather than what they want. People do not like to be reminded that they must eat their veggies and that their children must be disciplined. Instead, they write about how to effectively communicate with their children and which foods will help them lose weight. Simply changing the word "needs" to "wishes" will increase the number of people interested in your material. Simply asking people what they want will reveal their desires.

Writing an eBook that doesn't answer an issue is a waste of time. When consumers search online, they frequently have an issue that they want to fix right now. That's part of the allure of selling information on the internet: someone may search for a solution to their problem, come across your eBook, and buy it right away. Even if you're fast asleep halfway around the world, you can accomplish this.

You'll have a better chance of selling your eBook or other information product on the internet if you avoid these three blunders.

## Attempting to do everything on your own

You've finished writing your book, but it still has to be edited, proofread, typeset, and a cover designed. Don't try to do everything yourself, even if you're on a low budget. If you have grammatical errors or a self-indulgent ending, your book will not sell well or receive positive reviews. Hire an expert to proofread and edit your work. Even if this is your day job, you're too close to your work to be a competent editor and proofreader. It's possible to accomplish decent cover design, typesetting, and marketing on your own these days. Just be honest with yourself about whether or not you are capable of doing these tasks and whether or not you are knowledgeable enough about them. For instance, you'll need to create a book cover that looks nice both as a thumbnail and at a bigger size. It's worth outsourcing design and typesetting to a professional if you have the funds. This will save you time while also potentially increasing revenue. Another alternative is to debut your book on a shoestring budget and then reinvest the revenues in a new edition with more material and a more professional-looking design.

## Being too late with your market research

Don't only conduct market research while promoting your book. You don't want any unpleasant surprises, like finding out that another author has the same name or title as you. If you uncover problems like these early on, you can take steps to address them, such as changing your book title and using your middle name or a pseudonym. Early stage research also allows you to ensure that there is a market for your book, which will help you advertise it later. Even in fiction, this is true. Consider the following question: Who is your target market? What are they now reading? Where could they get such a book? Why do you think they'd read yours?

## Launching cold

It's simple to believe "My novel is now complete. All of the hard work has been completed." Unfortunately, this is not the case. Promoting your book is just as difficult, and it's something you should start doing even before you publish. Can you include your readers in the early stages of the writing and publishing process? This will aid in the development of interest and demand for your ebook. It also means you'll be able to establish an email list to use when you finally launch your ebook. After all, what could be better than sending out a mailing to folks who are already interested on your launch day and watching your sales numbers rise?

## Being too shy or scared to ask for reviews

If you get an email or a tweet from someone who likes your book, invite them to post an online review. This is especially crucial at the beginning, when early evaluations can have a big impact on whether or not someone buys your book. Early evaluations can have an impact on what other reviewers say. When everyone else enjoys a book, it's more difficult to give it a 2*. Your product launch should include a review approach. Make a list of people you'd like to review your book and offer them a (free) copy. Don't be alarmed if you get a few negative reviews. These can add credibility and show that your book is being reviewed by more than just your friends and family! You may be confident that you've created a good book that your intended audience will enjoy. If you have any reservations about the quality of your book, go back to mistake #1 and get a skilled editor!

## Forgetting traditional marketing methods.

Just because you've published an ebook doesn't mean you have to market it solely through social media. Traditional marketing strategies can still work. Work out how you may appear in a magazine that your target audience reads, for example. Give a talk or a workshop at your local library, book festival, or book club. It's not even necessary for you to read from your book. If you've produced a work of fiction with tarot reading as a motif, for example, you might be more likely to be granted publicity opportunities if you're willing to talk about a similar issue. People will listen to you if you portray yourself as someone who is engaged in and excited about a topic related to your ebook and eager to talk about it in an understandable manner. You can then tell them all about your book.

## Making it all about you

Because you've been so engrossed in your work, it's easy to fall into the habit of telling everyone you encounter about your book and why it's so fantastic. To some extent, this is beneficial since your passion will spread. However, don't pass up the opportunity to hear what others have to say about your book. Claire's readers provided her with some excellent suggestions for describing and marketing her book 52 Dates for Writers. They informed her what they liked and didn't like about the book, which she could utilize to better advertise it to her target demographic.

## Being suffocated by social media

Plan basic goals that you can achieve, such as promoting two blog posts on Twitter, Facebook, and Goodreads once a month. It's more vital to connect with social media on a regular basis than to start with a frenzy of activity and then produce simply a smattering of content as the months pass. It takes time to gain traction on social media, so don't get discouraged if you don't receive a lot of likes or follows right away. Also, keep in mind that social media is all about having fun! Claire incorporated the idea of community into her marketing campaign for her book 52 Dates for Writers by asking individuals to share writing they'd made from her book with her – and her followers.

## Having a shoddy sales page is a big no-no.

You've finished your ebook project and are ready to go on to the next step: selling it. Hold your horses! It's pointless to spend time promoting your ebook just to turn people off when they arrive at your sales page and see poor material, grammatical errors, and an untrustworthy author photo. Allow enough time to complete this section of the project. Consider having your editor work on both your book and your publicity materials; if you factor it in at the start, it shouldn't add too much to the project's cost. To get a good author portrait, hire a professional photographer or enlist the help of a talented friend.

**selling on insufficient platforms**

It's simple to come to a halt at Amazon. However, you should try to sell your book on a variety of channels, such as Amazon, Kobo, and Apple. You'll be able to reach out to a larger number of potential customers this way. Keep an open mind about new prospects as well. ePublishing is still a developing sector; tomorrow's participants may be completely different, and early adopters will benefit from staying on top of new distribution channels. Remember to launch it on your own website or blog as well! Amazon, for example, takes a large percentage of your income and only allows you to format your content in a certain way. You'll make more money on each transaction and be able to optimize your marketing text if you sell directly to readers. Of course, figuring out payment methods and securely and automatically delivering digital files to your readers isn't straightforward, which is where SendOwl comes in. We make it simple for you to sell ebooks online utilizing a short link from your website, blog, or social media.

Taking an excessive amount of time to produce your next ebook

After launching your ebook, you undoubtedly feel like you need a well-deserved vacation, but don't go too far! Keep in touch with your readers and don't make them wait too long for your next ebook, whether it's part of a series or something new. Consider whether you can supplement your ebooks with other digital offerings. Creating a Disgusting Cover

Think again if you think your eBook's cover isn't crucial. The cover not only introduces readers to the subject at hand, but it can also help you sell your eBook. In the worst-case scenario, a poorly designed cover may deter potential customers from purchasing your goods. Keep in mind, though, that even a mediocre cover design can detract from your book's success. An ugly cover can drastically hinder an eBook's selling potential when it's fighting for attention with dozens or hundreds of other books.

## Inconsistent branding

A good eBook may help you establish your business, and all of your items should work together to help you build your brand. Rather than developing your eBook in-house, hire a professional designer to give it the polish it requires to stand out as a credible product. A professional can guarantee that branding is consistent and successful not only in a single eBook, but also across a series or a product line.

## Making a Mistake by Using the Wrong Platform

Not all eBook platforms are made equal, and choosing the wrong one could result in you missing out on a slew of sales or excluding an entire market segment. The simplest approach for publication and distribution is to create an eBook in PDF format and sell it on your own website, but it isn't always the most profitable. Begin by evaluating the numerous Amazon choices and determining which can assist you in expanding your audience while also benefiting your bottom line. Don't overlook how selling your eBook on that platform will help you increase your sales and reputation.

Though Amazon is the most well-known name in publishing, it is far from the only major distribution route available to you. Consider some of the other large names, such as Apple or Barnes and Noble, which also have their own eBook platforms. Keep in mind that the eBook market is constantly changing, so make sure to use up-to-date resources to help you with your study.

## Absence of a marketing strategy

The majority of businesses do not create eBooks only to disseminate industry information. Instead, these items function as effective marketing tools that can be used to do everything from make a case for your company's products and services to position you as an expert in your sector. That's why it's critical to develop a marketing strategy long before you publish. Consider how you might advertise your eBook by developing a landing page, seeking reviews from experts in your industry, guest blogging on relevant sites, publishing similar material on your own site, and utilizing social media.

## Choosing a Price Point That Isn't Appropriate

Navigating an eBook, but for a variety of reasons, the price tag can make or break your eBook sales. Pricing that is too high will almost likely turn off some potential customers, and failing to evaluate the pricing of a competitor's goods will also hurt your sales. Pricing too low, on the other hand, can limit your return and put your investment at risk. Before deciding on a price point, conduct market research to learn about industry best practices and do the arithmetic to find your desired price point.

## Resources

### Book Distribution Services

If you're an indie author, navigating the logistics of self-publishing and distributing your work can be complicated. To make this complex process simpler, several services are available to help authors distribute their books:

Smashwords – offers easy book distribution to most of the world's largest ebook retailers (excluding Amazon) and thousands of libraries. They also provide free tools for marketing, metadata management, and sales reporting.

Draft2Digital – another option for ebook distribution. They handle formatting, while the author can easily set the price of their books, get monthly payments, and see daily book sales reports.

BookBaby – BookBaby offers book print on demand (POD), ebook distribution, and editing and design services for varying fees. They distribute to Amazon, although many authors prefer to work directly with Amazon instead.

Amazon Kindle Direct Publishing – Amazon KDP lets authors convert and distribute their ebooks for Kindle, and now offers POD. There are two options to publish directly on Amazon: KDP and KDP Select, which requires exclusive distribution through Amazon. CreateSpace has now merged with KDP.

IngramSpark – a POD platform and online publishing tool that provides access to Ingram's global distribution network for print and ebook content. It's a one-stop shop for print and ebook distribution, but has upfront costs and fees in addition to royalties.

## Cover Design Services

If you're on a tight budget, purchasing a premade book cover is a viable option as well. Here are a few options:

GoOnWrite – has hundreds of covers available across dozens of genres/topics, with pricing starting at $50 per cover with discounts for multiples. James, the designer of all of these covers, offers custom design services as well.

DIY Book Covers – at an $87 fee, access hundreds of book cover templates, plus some extras including interior layout templates, an ISBN Barcode Generator, and 3D renderings of the cover once it's ready.

Damonza – offers dozens of premade cover designs for $195 each, which includes minor changes to the font or colors. They also offer custom design services.

Paper & Sage Design – offers dozens of designs across many different genres for only $50 per cover (or $100 for a print + ebook bundle).

Littera Designs – has numerous covers available across many genres.

Cover Shot Creations – offers premade covers in romance, YA, new adult, sci-fi/fantasy, thriller/mystery, and western categories.

# Conclusion

Creating an ebook takes a lot of work and effort from beginning to end. If done correctly, though, a successful ebook can generate new leads for your company and establish your brand's competence in your field.

So, what do you have to lose?

Start by following our ebook writing tutorial to bring it to life. Just keep in mind that your ebook should be tailored to your specific business requirements.

That's it! You now have everything you need to write a successful eBook. I understand how frightening the prospect was at first. But with these simple steps and pointers, you'll not only have an eBook in no time, but one that's entertaining, generates discussion, and utterly rocks.